FROM COUCH TO MARATHON

FROM COUCH TO MARATHON

GRETA ROSE

CONTENTS

1	Introduction to Running	1
2	Getting Started	5
3	Building Endurance	9
4	Nutrition for Runners	13
5	Injury Prevention and Management	17
6	Mental Preparation	21
7	Training Plans	25
8	Race Day Tips	31
9	Recovery and Rest	35
10	Staying Motivated	39
11	Conclusion	43

Copyright © 2024 by Greta Rose
All rights reserved. No part of this book may be reproduced in any manner whatsoever without written permission except in the case of brief quotations embodied in critical articles and reviews.
First Printing, 2024

CHAPTER 1

Introduction to Running

Running is the most basic form of exercising, and one of the easiest ways to kick off a fitness routine. Whether you are a diehard gym buff or just want to get some fresh air and clear your mind after work, running is the best way to get your heart rate up and stay in shape. And the best part? No material is required, and joining a gym is not a must. But getting started and staying on course is usually the hard part. That's where I step in. In this series, I am going to show you what running is really about, how to get started, stay committed, and have fun.

Remember, all beginners are different. Running can be very easy for some and hard for others. I was one of those people who hated running, was slow, and never could build endurance. One mile into my run, and I was huffing and puffing. Two minutes into my run, and sweat poured down my face. It wasn't until after high school that I touched my first pair of sneakers and hit the dirt in my neighborhood. What seemed impossible at first became a regular routine of days and miles, and a second and third marathon. These words can also be your first step and serve as an inspiration. I am not trying to tell you to go sign up for the marathon. And I am not going to tell you that it is easy. But if you aren't satisfied with your progress, I will. And this guide is like a good friend who has the experience and is more than willing to keep you company. Running is not just physical, but a mental intensity sport. And the key to that intensity lies within.

Benefits of Running

Running is a physical activity that can be enjoyed by anyone at any age. Whether you're 20 or 70, each day someone starts running and lots of people continue to run well into their advanced years. They train, take part in races and have competitive goals. Running may not be for everyone but the undeniable health benefits of taking it up should make you think twice!

Are you thinking of taking up running but are not sure how to go about it? This helpful guide will show you in simple steps how to start running and how to progress gradually, how to get your basic gear in order, how to avoid getting injured and tips for staying motivated. It's no secret that any form of physical exercise is good for your body but running is one of the best. Not only does it help to keep you fit, running is guaranteed to reduce stress, clear the mind, help you sleep better, control your weight and generally make you feel great. Not only that, jogging outdoors is a wonderful way to discover your local area and enjoy the fresh air outside at the same time. Running is also a straightforward, democratic and very affordable sport. Once you start running all you need is a pair of running shoes and a bit of willpower. The other great thing about running is that age is no barrier.

Setting Realistic Goals

A simpler, more realistic goal for a beginner might be to lose a few pounds after several weeks of steady running. Then, after you run your first five minutes without stopping, you can set a goal of running eight minutes without stopping. Then it's fifteen. And from there your goals could become distance or race specific. Your goals need to be realistic for you. Make your goals attainable and achievable and you are more likely to continue running... and more goals will be met because you continue. When setting your goals, remember to trust your body, eat healthily, and get plenty of rest. Your body will tell you when and how often you should run. And listen to it. That advice will not only keep you running, but it will also help prevent you from getting hurt.

First of all, congratulations on making the decision to start running. This is the first and most important step. Once you have made that decision, your next big step is to decide what you want to achieve with your running. Many beginners set unrealistic goals, such as losing an excessive amount of weight right from the start, or running fifteen miles a day every day. This doesn't mean that you can't lose a large amount of weight or run fifteen miles every day. It just means that for most of us, a more gradual progression usually works better and is more sustainable.

CHAPTER 2

Getting Started

Many middle- and long-distance training guides would suggest that you have an aerobic endurance base upon which to build before starting your marathon training. I also suggest this too, but one should note that this base does not have to come solely from running. Activities such as fast walking and bicycling are also excellent ways to develop the needed heart and skeleton-muscular systems that running a marathon demands. If you can integrate various stress-reducing activities to be shared with running such as swimming, stretching, and yoga, you would be better off and find yourself less prone to injury in addition to being more refreshed. Whatever non-running workouts you choose, their goal should be to give your heart and bones and muscles the work they need without making you feel exhausted, stressed, or excessively fatigued.

It is important to note that you should not jump out of the couch and begin by running a marathon. You must be patient and keep in mind that getting in peak running shape takes time. Even if you have been exercising and can easily take 30 or 60-minute walks, launching headlong into running can lead to overuse injuries, extra soreness, and more mental anguish than may be necessary!

Choosing the Right Gear

Approved running shoes and socks can also contribute to preventing this discomfort. Use specialized stores to evaluate your foot form correctly and notice your behavior when running so they can provide the best socks. Some jogging gear will make your run more pleasant, though luxury is not necessary. Even technical gear, such as running clothes, is necessary in the chilly air. Reflective details on night events offer protection. It sounds fantastic in essence and may save you after you've eventually crossed the main milestone in race training. Runners at specific retail stores typically have such a relation. Consider trying it for a week, an adjustment period for your overall body. Run in small stretches initially and walk instead of running up if you lack the strength.

Choosing the right shoes is very important. You are more likely to put it off over sore feet than injury, so invest in a pair of good quality running shoes. Go to a specialist store where knowledgeable staff can analyze your stride and running style to help you select the best shoes for you. The right style will prevent injury and protect your knees and orthopedic joint replacements. Try wearing a few models and brands in the store to get a feel for the perfect ones for your foot shape and running mechanics. For professional advice, it is worth consulting a podiatrist who can screen your foot shape and make orthopedic insoles that suit it. Everyone has variations in the length of their legs and should be able to have these insoles prescribed.

Proper Running Form

When running, always try to hold your arms in loose fists at a 90-degree angle as they swing. Your arms should be pumping and propelling you forward! Your feet should land directly under your center of gravity, and when they fall you should be leaning slightly forward. The feet should fall straight and lightly strike the ground and push you off behind you.

Your form is very important so you do not injure yourself. Good form will also use your energy more efficiently. To run properly, lift your body and feel your posture becoming totally straight. Good alignment is absolutely necessary for an effective and injury-free running experience. Your body should be tall, your ears should be level with your shoulders, your abs should be sucked in, your pelvis should be rotated slightly forwards, and your arms should hang comfortably from your shoulders. Do not clench your fists, and try to relax your shoulders and your hands. All of these steps should ideally place you in a 'neutral' position which will decrease injury and strain on the body while running.

CHAPTER 3

Building Endurance

But the good news is that you can build endurance relatively easily and without any major long-term impacts on your life. You've got a couple of things in your favor. First, your heart and lungs are adaptable: they quickly become stronger and less flabby. Second, and the more interesting part (at least in my opinion), you have a special kind of muscle fiber, called a slow-twitch fiber, that's designed specifically for sustained endurance activity. Everyone has these special fibers to some degree; some of us just have more than others. Fortunately, you can increase the number of slow-twitch fibers in your body, although you will first need to train them - and the easiest way to 'train' these fibers is actually by using them to do frequent, but less intense workouts. In essence, you're training your body to replace fat with muscle, to exchange capillaries that carry waste products away from your muscles for more efficient and effective ones, to strengthen your hip, knee, and ankle joints, and to become better at moving your body in a coordinated and efficient way. And each time you train, you're increasing the system's capacity to deliver. The result: you become better.

Endurance is, of course, a key aspect of running, and one that many new runners (including, or rather especially, those who are otherwise in great shape) find challenging at the start. People imagine that running is strictly about the legs, but they couldn't be more wrong. In fact, your legs can quickly build the ability to carry your body for a very long time (indeed, better than just about any other part of the body, legs adapt very quickly). But if you've had a sedentary lifestyle, it's important to remember that your heart and respiratory system - the two systems that work together to carry oxygen and nutrients to the body's cells, and to transport cellular waste products away for disposal - are very, very weak, and that they will quickly become exhausted if you try to do too much, too soon. The end result will be that you feel as though you're completely out of breath, and that your legs don't want to do what you're asking them to do. After that happens, your brain will very quickly step in and say, "Whoa, Nelly!", and then all you're going to want to do is lie down, and give up on the idea of running altogether.

Gradual Progression

The reasons for not starting too enthusiastically are many. The first is that strong and durable legs can be built faster than strong tendons, bones, and the other less endurance-oriented muscles and tissues. If you can manage increasing the demands on your body while it is adjusting to the exercise, you will find you will be able to run faster and longer than if you take the slow, steady approach, but there is a high risk of injury. After each consecutive period of intense exercise, your body will need a longer time to return to its base level.

Many people can already walk for an hour, and that can make you feel like running should be much the same experience. Those thoughts might lead you into starting out too intensely, feeling tired and sore, then giving up. In order to adapt, recover, and progress with minimized risk of injury, there is nothing wrong with walking your way through the intervals if needed. The way I generally suggest people to progress, except for the absolute beginners, is by a weekly

10% increase in total training time. At some point, the slow increase will mean that there will need to be some weeks with more or less the same amount of time running, with an increase in volume some time later, but for newcomers to the sport, this is not really an issue.

Incorporating Cross-Training

For your first 3-4 months of training, keep your long run at a slow, easy pace which you can converse at least every other week. The goal is to build your endurance and strength. Going too fast early on may lead to injury or become too stressful for your body and mind, which will eventually affect your running career. The great thing about easy runs is they stress different energy systems and muscles in your body. Speed workouts certainly get you in better shape, but without the proper base being established, they can't perform their role as well.

Although your primary goal is to become a better runner, don't let other aspects of your fitness fall by the wayside. Additionally, doing something else active or attending a workout class is a great way to have a bit of a flexible routine. For me, cross-training keeps me looking forward to doing something else active. However, it has this great effect of slowly building muscles in your legs that running can neglect. These muscles can help prevent injury, so it's important to keep them in shape.

CHAPTER 4

Nutrition for Runners

Rethink Your Carbs. Running means carbs, right? Ten years ago you'd be correct, sir. Something special happened - a little race called The New York City Marathon went by and shifted what runner's thoughts are on dipping into fuel. A few years ago, carb gels, goos, and energy blocks weren't a racer's choice. Nowadays, let's face the facts - they can be really good friends to have during races, especially at mile 18 of a marathon. Behind door number one we have runners who drink an extra 16-24 ounces of fluid with their energy sources. Behind door number two we have runners who also carry an extra sprinkle of salt (insert girl joke here). After energy boosts, pounds are immediately restored - critically refueling the body.

Mind the Mini-Meal. For runners, planning three full meals a day just isn't going to properly nourish your body. Focus on integrating one or two extra mini-meals in the mix. Eat a snack like an apple with cheese one to two hours before a meal to keep digestive issues from being a problem. Slams the door on a wall of fatigue. Small meals keep energy levels consistent without creating hunger or weight issues. Skipping meals does not an ideal runner make.

When runners put precious time and energy into training, they want to see visible and encouraging results. Focusing on not only your running plan, but also nutrition, properly fueling your body is the missing factor that's going to lead to those great times. Without fuel, performance goes seriously downhill. And no thank you! To maximize results, integrate these easy eating habits into your diet.

Pre-Run Fueling

Eating, or not, before a run is a personal choice that can depend on several factors including your energy needs, your metabolic responses to food, the types of workouts you're doing, personal preference, and your body's ability to adapt to training on an empty stomach. Some people prefer running or working out on an empty stomach because it can reduce the risk of gastrointestinal distress. Others want to ensure they have plenty of fuel in their tanks for running hard and optimally. Much of this depends on the time of day you run or work out and your personal digestion time. Many runners also feel like they can run faster and more comfortably if they've eaten something. Most humans go into a fasted state overnight, and when you wake in the morning, your body is typically in a fasted state, in which your body is burning fewer carbohydrates and more fat than it would during the day, when you're in a fed state. This is the metabolic state which some people refer to when talking about "burning fat." A light carbohydrate and protein-rich snack, in particular, can give you a needed energy boost while providing ideal muscle fuel to get you out the door and through a workout, so long as you tolerate it and do not experience any gastrointestinal distress once you begin running.

Post-Run Recovery

Running and any other physical exercise can take its toll on the body, but there are a few things you can do in order to benefit. The sooner after exercising, the more effective these strategies can be. We will go through each one in the order they typically occur.

1. Immediate recovery. This stage is especially valuable for intense workouts during which lactic acid or other metabolic waste has built up in your muscles, or after long runs that slightly damage your muscle fibers. A reduction of metabolic waste or beginning the repair process quickly can help prevent the pain and residual muscle soreness that often occurs a day or two after the workout. After you finish your run, you can help speed up recovery by walking and/or stretching immediately. This allows your muscles to begin the relaxation and waste removal. It also helps to bring your heart rate down more gradually, which is easier on your circulatory system. Eating some form of high-glycemic carbohydrate in the first half hour after your workout helps replenish spent muscle glycogen.

2. Over the next two hours. Especially after long or intense sessions, your metabolism will remain high even though you've stopped running. Your muscles are replacing lost glycogen and the protein repair process for muscle fibers is also working at peak levels, burning more calories than usual. Eating more carbohydrates in this window of time can help speed up glycogen replacement, while protein will help to repair the damage to muscle fibers. Also, don't forget that the entire time within the first 24- to 48-hour period after exercise is when heightened intake of water, protein, amino acids, or antioxidants may help the most in your ongoing recovery process. This is also a great time to relax in a hot bath or hot tub.

3. Recovery massage. Taking it easy after running can often feel counterintuitive—restless or antsy. Some runners find that a relaxing, light gentle massage soothes active muscles when they are in this hyper-receptive post-exercise state, allowing them to relax comfortably ahead of their next workout. If you're going to receive a post-run massage, this is the time to do it. Autocorrective treatments and an emphasis on recycling a runner's muscle waste will make the massage far more beneficial. Tissue will be more receptive longer.

Remember that at its most fundamental level, overcoming the fatigue caused by physical exercise is what recovery is all about. By following a few simple practices, you can enhance your body's natural recovery process and head back out on the track or trail with confidence.

CHAPTER 5

Injury Prevention and Management

Preventing Injuries
Before we finish up, it seems there's one last incredibly important topic we've yet to discuss when it comes to running: preventing injuries. When you're starting out, there are some golden rules to follow to ensure you make it through your early stages of running injury-free so that you can enjoy running and plan for bigger goals unhindered further down the line.

First off, the biggest mistake new runners tend to make is doing too much too soon. Yes, you're running a lot less than your friends who've been at it for longer, but your friends didn't get there overnight. One incredibly common mistake is increasing speed and distance when your body is still adapting - the result is usually injury. Another area to be careful about is old and second-hand running shoes. Your trainers are your most important piece of kit when it comes to running. If your soles are worn down, especially under your heel, forefoot, and big toe, it's very possible that you're at a much higher risk of injuries. Making sure you have good shoes that give you maximum support and cushioning as you take the impact will go a long way into preventing injuries.

Common Running Injuries

Runners often develop injuries from the constant impact and repetitive motion of the exercise. However, following the proper safety precautions, such as wearing properly cushioned shoes, should help to prevent the majority of injuries. The most common injury areas are:

Knee: Most running injuries include knee pain. These misalignments can be the result of weak or unbalanced leg muscles, an overly tight inner thigh muscle (the abductor), or even simply excessive strain on the joint.

Hip: Tension in the iliotibial rubber band structure often causes hip pain among runners. This is a long section running down the outside of the thigh. This rubbing irritation frequently causes bursitis, a painful inflammation of the hip.

Foot: Blisters on the feet can be caused by ill-fitting socks and/or poorly fitting shoes. Shin splints are pain found inside the shin bone. The front section of the lower leg often is subject to terrible pain during a workout, signaling a probable case of shin splints. The stress can even induce a consistent ache throughout the entire day.

Calf: The Achilles tendon or the foot's heel is the basis for this injury. Soleus and gastrocnemius tendons are also common to this injury. If any of these muscles are tight, walking could be very painful. Keep well-stretched or else inflammation is likely to exist.

Hamstring: The back section of your thigh is a common site for a hamstring injury. Treat the ache with RICE solution or time off if the muscle overwhelms you.

Groin: The inner area of your thigh often experiences ache when groined. Athletic training courses can include stretching exercises to facilitate healing.

Back: Most of our body's weight rests on the spinal cord. The waves produced during running transmit right through this section.

At times, the body might counterbalance the stress with immense force, throwing it directly back to the lumbar spine. This can cause a dull ache and pains in the legs and glutes.

Bursitis cures: These fluid-filled sacs are commonly inflamed during running. They are created to ease the flow of all muscles near joints and eliminate friction produced from rubbing against each other. When these sacs grow too big, they can become inflamed. Cooling the area will help treat this injury. Do not aggravate the sore area. If these symptoms do not improve, then physical therapy or at a minimum a consultation from a physician will be essential.

Stretching and Mobility Exercises

Before diving into that bending and stretching action, here are a few things to keep in mind about stretching. Personally, I like to stretch post-run, as it often leaves me feeling fresh and relaxed. However, it's good to remember that dynamic stretches (like high knees) are best to complete before you start your run because static stretching (like a hamstring stretch) when your muscles are cold can cause muscle strain. Static stretching is best to incorporate post-run or as a separate routine. If (like me!) you're a newcomer to the stretching game and struggle with where to start, I often look to for tips on how to introduce mobility exercises and foam rolling into my routine. Amoila's guide to post-run stretching and Frank's guide to mobility exercises are two of my current resources. Do you currently use a stretching or mobility routine to help support your running? Is there a resource that you swear by and you think I should check out too?

So you've begun your running journey, but you've noticed that you feel tight and are moving with a bit more effort than you did before you began running. Does this sound familiar? Incorporating a stretching routine has many benefits for your running performance, including increasing the range of motion in your hips and lengthening muscles that tend to tighten (like your hamstrings, quadriceps, and calves). This can translate to smoother and more powerful movements when you run. For me, I like to be proactive rather than reactive and often include a range of mobility exercises in my runs or as a separate routine throughout the week to help reduce the likelihood of injury.

CHAPTER 6

Mental Preparation

The good news is that, as you improve, many of these alarming sensations will almost completely disappear, and they'll be replaced with a calming calmness as you realize that running tests your body, soul, and nerves like no other sport can do. In its own way, running can be immensely liberating. First, let's talk about that feeling - the "I want to quit" reflex. You'll begin to recognize it after a very short period of running, when the muscles in your legs start to become tired. You'll feel it later on, when running at an easy pace over a longer distance, that requires you to persist in order to complete the goal. When beginners confront this feeling, the first solutions to running are quit. After all, it's not like our ancestors would have evaded a hunting animal for more than a few minutes (remember, we're still animals - a dog is faster than an Olympic sprinter, albeit for not nearly as long).

When you are a beginner runner, running any distance will require you to do something counterintuitive - be comfortable with being uncomfortable (or, at least, standing on the edge of discomfort). Yep, you have to accept that running really isn't all that easy. Sometimes it's reassuring to learn that all runners, no matter how fast or efficient, will come face-to-face with discomfort eventually. The difference is how they react to the symptoms. If you are just starting out, read this - that feeling where you feel like stopping - this may be the most important lesson you learn in your early running days. This is the feeling that, if you stop, will never transform your body or mental toughness.

Mindfulness and Focus Techniques

Podcasts - It is possible to listen to podcasts while running, even on sidewalks. Use headphones on a low volume setting. There are a number of fitness, educational, and humor podcasts to entertain or distract. Music is not mentioned in this category. Almost all runners love music. Bring enough for variety. Choose an easy to use MP3 player and keep it up to date with a wide range of music styles. Keep the volume low and consider only using one earbud at a time. Make sure it is secure and cannot fall out while running.

Other than keeping a safe pace and injury prevention, running very long distances like a marathon includes the challenge of dealing with the boredom. Your legs get tired and start to hurt; a distraction changes the focus from how hard they are working. This is completely normal and makes up for nearly half the mental challenge of finishing. Distractions are needed to keep the mind fighting throughout the entire event. Anything to stop boredom from rotting your determination to keep going. So, experiment with a few of the following techniques to find which one gives the most comfort to your mind.

Dealing with Setbacks

In addition to the tips listed here, any injury's best friend is biking. Since biking does not create the ground shock that leg muscles are damaged by, it is often a good way for runners to continue to train. The precise diagnosis of what's wrong and what should be done about it is normally in the hands of a doctor or physical therapist. They may suggest changes in your routines to do two things: exercise and ice, and rest and repeat.

Pain in the knees, ankles, or feet: Trying out new shoes may give you some insight into the cause of the pain. If you get the wrong feeling, the foot isn't very well. Listen to your feelings and find a pair of shoes between them.

Muscle cramps or soreness: It's better to prevent soreness than to try to cure it. You don't have to run each workout as intensely as you can. Take care to avoid any sudden bursts of fast running in the middle of slow running.

Inflammation: Reddened, swollen, painful to touch, and may have a dull ache. Applying the Ice Treatment you learned in the first section is often very effective in relieving inflammation.

Bone Injury: Often feels better when you don't run on it. Causes for the pain are normally either some kind of stress fracture or severe inflammation in the tendons around the bone. In the worst case, the tendon snaps. Any pain indicating bone injury is serious and should not be ignored. Ignoring them may lead to weeks off rather than days.

Hopefully, the information up to now will help you stay healthy and keep running. But most runners do have at least occasional setbacks. Here are a few of the most common problems:

CHAPTER 7

Training Plans

The Beginner Programs are designed to help new runners and those who are returning to running after a period of time off get started from the base level of being able to run just 30 seconds at a time. Most users of the program will include a substantial number of walks as well as runs in their workout, but for those who find the workout too easy, the time of individual run/walk segments can be easily adjusted. The primary guideline for preparations is common sense. The Intermediate Running Programs are designed for those runners who have already finished or who already have experience at the 5K or 10K running distances and for those who are choosing to start running again after a period of inactivity. Those runners just finishing the Beginner Running Program are ideal candidates to initiate the Intermediate Running Programs. However, for those runners finding the Intermediate program too easy, in each of the eight weeks of the program, one may be able to verify the physical changes of training, according to the schedule provided by the program, by simply skipping over that week to the next harder week of training. These running programs are harder and require longer running time. All runners are different and are able to respond differently to the stress of running. Some will need the full eight-week program of gradually more difficult running to reach a faster, trained running pace. Others, who start with a ready level of physical and mental toughness, can reach the same level of running, possibly in less time. In either case, upon reaching the ability to complete the level Eighth Week Intermediate run or the Fourteenth Week Intermediate run, you will be ready to continue on these programs toward the next running goal - the 10K or the half marathon.

I have included three different types of running programs - a Beginner's, Intermediate, and a Marathon Running Program. There are many pre-made running programs available for purchasing, but you can save some hard-earned money by using one of my programs or use them as a base and change as required. I polled several runners from the Running II section of the Runners World Forums and asked them what they liked and disliked about the running programs included in this guide. All of the runners loved the running programs. They praised the programs for the great variety and expressed that the programs really helped to keep running fun. The runners also loved that the running programs taught them much about general training and running. The programs are designed to make gradual improvements in your running performance and to keep your mind as well as your running body happy. If you want a good workout and want to get the most out of your training time, stretch both before and after the workout. This is really important, but it is sometimes the most ignored part of a runner's day.

5K Training Plan

The plan has you running for at least 20 minutes, three times a week, at an easy conversational pace. Each week, the intensity of your runs—the fourth in the first week, the third in the second week, the second in the third week, and the first in the fourth through seventh weeks—increases. For the runs that aren't the focus of the week, feel free to walk or split the distance with walking. On one day a week, you'll cross-train, doing any kind of exercise that's not running. Stretching after any workout is also key. Each running session includes a five-minute warm-up walk at the beginning and end, followed by five minutes of cool down walking. Make sure you're hydrating well before and after you run, paying close attention to your body's cues. And if you have any additional injury or health concerns, consult your healthcare provider before starting this (or any) workout routine.

The following 5K training plan is based on one that running coach and exercise physiologist Susan Paul developed with beginner runners in mind. The goal is to gradually prepare the body to handle the 3.1-mile distance. The plan spans just eight weeks—short enough to be attainable but long enough for you to prep your muscles and your heart for running. It is designed for individuals who have been walking or running for two weeks or more and can comfortably walk for 30 minutes.

10K Training Plan

Here is an intermediate 10k training schedule based around the 5k I have already covered. I am assuming a finish time between 30-60 minutes for 10k.

Weeks: 1-6 Hours: Below 90 minutes Runs: up to 5

Week 1 Day 1: Rest or XT (Cross Training) Day 2: 1 mile easy, 4 x 20s max w/ 20s recovery, 1 mile easy Day 3: 0.5 mile-2 mile easy Day 4: Rest or XT Day 5: 1 mile easy w/ 2 x 20s max in last minute Day 6: Rest – get shoes Day 7: 1 mile easy

Week 2 Day 1: Rest or XT (Cross Training) Day 2: 1 mile easy, 4 x 20s max w/ 20s recovery, 1 mile easy Day 3: 0.5 mile-2 mile easy Day 4: Rest or XT Day 5: 1 mile easy w/ 2 x 20s max in last minute Day 6: Rest Day 7: 1 mile easy w/ 2 x 20s max in last minute

Week 3 Day 1: Rest or XT Day 2: 1 mile easy, 4 x 20s max w/ 20s recovery, 1 mile easy Day 3: 0.5 mile-2 mile easy Day 4: Rest or XT Day 5: 1 mile easy w/ 2 x 20s max in last minute Day 6: Rest Day 7: 1 mile easy w/ 2 x 20s max in last minute

Week 4 Day 1: Rest or XT Day 2: 1 mile easy, 4 x 20s max w/ 20s recovery, 1 mile easy Day 3: 0.5 mile easy Day 4: Rest or XT Day 5: 1 mile easy w/ 2 x 20s max in last minute Day 6: Rest Day 7: 1 mile easy w/ 2 x 20s max in last minute

Week 5 Day 1: Rest or XT Day 2: 1 mile easy, 4 x 20s max w/ 20s recovery, 1 mile easy Day 3: Rest or XT Day 4: 1 mile easy w/ 2 x 20s max in last minute Day 5: Rest or XT Day 6: 2 mile easy w/ 2 x 20s max in last minute Day 7: Rest or XT

Week 6 Day 1: 0.5 mile easy Day 2: 1 mile easy, 6 x 20s max w/ 20s recovery, 0.5 mile easy Day 3: Rest or XT Day 4: 1 mile easy w/ 30s max in last minute Day 5: Rest or XT Day 6: 2 mile easy w/ 3 x 20s max in last minute Day 7: Rest or XT

Half Marathon Training Plan

The short answer is 'yes.' But at the same time, it's not a walk in the park. You should prepare to face some hard work and potentially hit what we call 'the wall.' But on the flipside, there's lots of fun, laughter, and enjoyment that comes with training for a half marathon too, just like any good adventure. First-timers, runners who want to comfortably run the entire distance, and those who are focused on a conservative time goal can all use the same training plan. Pace is a critical aspect of the half marathon, so get comfortable running during both your long and short runs at your goal pace. Come race day, it's about running smart and in your comfort zone. That may mean minimizing walking breaks and skipping water stations to maintain your speed. No matter what your goal pace, running smart is the key. Enjoy the challenge and have fun covering the distance with pride. The hard work you put in today will stay with you long after you cross the finish line. It's a big, hairy, audacious goal, but you can do it. So what are you waiting for, ask yourself, 'Why not?'

Running a half marathon is an ideal step up from a 10k. It's the perfect distance for runners who have conquered a 5k and 10k and are hungry to aim for more. It's also a useful step on the way to the ultimate challenge of a marathon or ultramarathon. On this page, you'll find our 16-week half marathon training plans, which are designed to help you reach the finish with confidence and enjoyment. But before you jump into the plan and start logging those miles, consider this: All it takes is a few simple steps. Just like any great running adventure, all it takes is a simple training plan, the right gear, a good pair of running shoes, and a little support. We offer a simple and easy-to-use training plan that will get you to the finish line of your half marathon feeling good.

Marathon Training Plan

The key to your success in finishing the marathon is to really dig down deep here and get it done. Much like the 10k and half marathon plans I have provided throughout this tutorial, I have begun with four easy runs a week. In the 16-week part of the schedule, you train for 12 weeks and the 4 weeks before the marathon you taper down to prepare your legs and body for the upcoming run. Again, I would strongly encourage everyone to get the book "Run Less, Run Faster" and discover why cross training and a proven marathon program can lead to superior performance, with less stress and problems.

So you think that you are ready to run a marathon? I hope so, because it is pretty easy to find a marathon to train for, but it is a much more difficult task to train your body for a 26.2 mile run. The following table contains a 12-week training schedule for beginners. It is a 20-week schedule with the first 8 weeks regular easy runs to build up your mileage, then the next 12 weeks are part of a 16-week marathon training schedule. Spend the first four weeks running a gentle treadmill run and taking it easy.

CHAPTER 8

Race Day Tips

The most important tips for first-time marathoners include starting slow, drinking at every water stop, eating lots of Jell-O, and most of all, entering the race for the right reasons. By now you should be figuring out some basic principles for a successful marathon. These are big things and by all means, pay attention to them because then you must take care of the little things. Here are our top tips for success to a perfect marathon race. Just by reading these tips, you gain excellent preparation and insight into the marathon itself. It can seem overwhelming in the beginning, and we hope to eliminate that kind of thought. The adrenaline might make you feel that you could run a 5:00 pace, do not do that, you could regret it later in the marathon. People are passed at the start line, but you will see many of them around you again, walking a few hours later in the marathon. Keep your eyesight in what is happening in front of you, but don't try to overtake everybody. Run your rhythm and goal and everything will be all right.

Pre-Race Preparation

The most important thing to remember is to dress according to how you're going to feel once you get warmed up. It's your choice, but do a good warm-up about 15 minutes before the start. The 5k,

8k, and 10ks are essentially the same type of race, and you should warm up the same for each. You won't be very fatigued or sweat too much if you do this, and you will be really and understandably ready to dash off the line.

It's hard to predict the weather and show up feeling great walking around in wet running shorts. Tissue paper is the answer. Don't let the weather dictate your running attire. If there's a steady rain in the morning, bring a garbage bag to the starting line. It will catch all the rain before the start, and you can discard it only after you've crossed the starting line. One year, I forgot about it and was soon soaked from head to toe. A garbage bag makes a good pre-race raincoat, complete with a hood, and it breathes. It also carries your numbers while you warm up and serves as a super souvenir if you don't throw it away. Take a pick-up throw-away at the school and put it in your gear bag for the start of the race. Carry your running clothes in a trash bag or under a big umbrella until a few minutes before the gun.

During the Race Strategies
Race Day Strategies

When it comes to the day of the race, the only real advice is to relax. Sounds silly, but this is where racing becomes the most fun. If you followed your training plan and are not trying to run faster than you are capable of running, all you have to do is relax and enjoy the journey. You will be running with hundreds or thousands of other runners, some faster, some slower. It is important to run your race and not worry about what others are doing. Your goal should be to be able to finish the race; you did not run all these weeks of training just to get caught up in the excitement of the start and collapse before the finish line was in sight. Stand in the middle of the pack at the beginning of the race; if you are faster than those around you, you will pass them, and if they are faster, they will pass you.

During the Race: Hydration and Nutrition

If only the race were like running 15 minutes and being done, but no, you will be out there for hours! How you eat and drink will greatly impact how well you will be able to perform. Drink at every aid station, but please do not try to drink all your water all at once. Take your time; you could walk to drink it; a little water will go a long way in keeping you hydrated. Depending on the weather, you should aim to drink at least 15-20 ounces of fluid per hour. You should also be consuming 100-250 calories each hour. If the race offers sports drink, you may alternate between that and water. I offer various gels and sport beans, but I suggest sticking to what you have consumed during your training. Feel free to bring your favorite snacks and drinks from home, but the race organization may not allow you to leave any containers or trash behind.

CHAPTER 9

Recovery and Rest

Another great workout to do is yoga to help with flexibility and recovery. Make sure you have at least 2 days a week of total rest, especially as a beginner. As a beginner, you are doing more work in terms of mileage compared to more experienced runners on a smaller base, so your body is adjusting more. As we progress through the plan, there will be recovery weeks which happen about once a month in order to give your body even more time to recover and reduce the risk of over-training. Make sure to take these weeks easier, as the easier weeks are when your body super-compensates and absorbs all this training.

Finally, let's discuss the most important part of training - recovery. Rest and recovery are the most important aspects of your training plan. Recovery allows your body time to repair itself and prevent the risk of over-training. The #1 rule for beginners is to make sure to take at least 2 rest days per week. Try to take your easier runs easier and your hard workouts hard. If you are running by effort levels, you should have a "conversational pace" where you are comfortable breathing and talking. It should feel easy, and "hard effort" should feel like you are pushing yourself but still in control. The recovery is significantly more important than the workouts as it is when your body adapts to the training. Finally, sleep is crucial, as this is when the body releases growth hormone and other anabolic hormones, so you need to give it the proper time to sleep. The main component of recovery is to give your body the time it needs to make these adaptations. The worse your recovery is, the more prone you are to injury, illness, and over-training.

Importance of Rest Days

Active recovery is another component of rest days. Active recovery is a workout at a very slow and easy pace. The lead legs don't apply as much force on your lead leg. They're highly recommended. It improves circulation and nutrient delivery, increases waste product removal, reduces soreness, reduces fatigue, increases your VO2 max, and increases capillary formation. The emphasis is on slow breathing. You should be able to carry on a conversation and breathe normally while running. If you can't carry on a conversation or breathe normally, then you're going too hard.

Rest days are another key element of your training plan. Your muscles actually never get stronger while you're working out. The rest and recovery are necessary to rebuild and repair the muscles that you've damaged while working out. You aren't building muscle when you're working out; you're breaking muscle down. You build muscle after your workout as you're recovering. It's perfectly fine to be sore for a day or 2 after a workout, but it's not fine to be so sore that you're unable to function and that you alter your stride. The only time it's okay to run on a sore or damaged muscle is if you're in a race, it's strictly for training, or it's after you've fully recovered. Working out also puts stress on your joints. This stress causes small areas of damage. The recovery time allows the joints to rebuild these small damaged areas before new stress is applied.

Recovery Techniques

Aside from being mentally beneficial after a tough workout, ice reduces inflammation, relieves swelling and soreness. The benefits of ice baths are mainly psychological. Although coaches and athletes swear by the rejuvenating benefits, there is little scientific evidence to support the claims. Many believe it has a placebo effect, although many will go out of their way to put one together. If you have the facilities to do one yourself, then it certainly cannot hurt, but people have been known to have a hose down (cold one) after long runs and races just to hasten the recovery.

Different people have different psychological responses to rest and recovery. Some will feel guilty and believe that by resting the training will be lost, while others know it will not happen and they need the rest and recovery time to maximize the builds they have experienced. Remember, if the rest is taken as a result of injury, this can translate to much more of a decline in form.

It is crucial that a beginner has a good recovery regime. Take it easy and have some rest for at least 24-48 hours after a long distance, even a marathon. Usually, there is no need to run the full distance of the event as part of your training program. A shorter distance, at three-quarter pace, is fine. You taper as you approach the big day, so your body has a chance to rejuvenate, repair and replace the energy lost during training.

CHAPTER 10

Staying Motivated

Countering negative thoughts is hard, but it's not too difficult if you believe that you have every right to be successful. Talk yourself into success. Your body won't go where your mind is not prepared to take it. If you don't intend to go to work, then stay home. If you don't intend on finishing the marathon training program, then don't even start. People often reject the reality of becoming injured while training for the marathon because the possibility generates a feeling of powerlessness. Others deny the reality of the potential mental and emotional struggles that can accompany marathon preparation. They think they are alone, that no one else in the population has problems staying disciplined with regard to diet or has to struggle to stay motivated toward the end of a very long training run. The fact that everyone else feels the same helps no one—then the diabetic feels he needs to eat a carbohydrate-based meal, and newcomers feel embarrassed about walking while running. Our feelings and responses to those feelings drive our training. When it comes to marathon training, all human beings are very much alike.

If I've said it once, I've said it a thousand times. Consistency and slow, incremental mileage increases are key in successful marathon training. Mental and emotional fitness play into it too. Pave the path to success by taking steps to clear the mind of worldly concerns. Of course, what this means varies greatly from person to person. Surround yourself, in person or virtually, with positive people. Spending time with people who believe in you will help you believe in yourself. Find times of day or specific locations to use for decompression and reflection. Keep a training journal and make daily entries. Self-questioning often leads to self-knowledge.

Finding Running Communities
Where to find running communities:
- Couchto5k: A community on Reddit that focuses on people training for their first 5k. - MarathonTraining: A community on Reddit that focuses on long distance running and marathons. - The Running Bug: A UK-based running community that includes blogs, running groups, and races. - Runner's World: Runner's World is the most popular running magazine. They offer online training programs, forums, online communities, and race information. - Meetup: Meetup.com lists numerous running groups, including trail running, social running, wellness and fitness groups that run, and groups that train for different races of varying distances. - Charity Running Organizations: Training with a charity is a great way to meet like-minded people, help out a charity in the process, and get a guaranteed spot in a race. The most popular programs are Team In Training, The LIVESTRONG Program, and the Susan G. Komen Race for the Cure.

How to find running communities:
- Do a search online for running communities and events in your area. - Check out online forums such as Reddit, Runner's World, and UltraRunning for running communities organized by activities of interest. - Go to Meetup.com and enter keywords such as running, marathon, 5k, race, and trail run in the search bar. - Follow a

well-known running training program, like Couchto5k, and run on your local running trails, in a park, or on your local running path. - Join a local gym as many of them have running communities that use a group to motivate each member to train. - Contact a personal trainer to see if they know of any running clubs or interested parties for training purposes. - Attend racing events to meet running clubs and organizations, and sign up for their programs if approved.

Setting New Goals

These are a few of the options available. The key to setting new goals is simply to decide on what to run for the fun and thrill of running. Enjoy (pg. 145).

Run for a charity. Running for a charity can add new meaning and purpose to a marathon.

Mentor a new runner. A person's first marathon is a monumental achievement. You share a common goal and bond that is difficult for others to offer support. Some of these new friendships turn into life-long running friends.

Travel to different marathons. There are so many beautiful courses all over the country and the world. Why not plan on seeing some of them while running a marathon?

Go for a PR (personal record or personal best). You can pick out a marathon and train to get a better finish time. Many of Black Hills Runner's Club members have run 35 to 50 marathons. They still try to get a PR. Just finishing a marathon and waiting for certificates to arrive in the mail can become somewhat lacking in motivation.

Acclimate to a new climate. You may have your eye on another marathon, but this one is in a different climate. No matter how great your marathon experience may have been, why not plan on a new adventure in a different city, state, or country?

Pacing another marathon. It can be great fun to pace a marathon and to help someone else achieve their goal.

You have completed a marathon. Now what? There is a phenomenon called PMS, or Post-Marathon Syndrome, that afflicts many runners. After a goal has been met, the object of all of their training and dreams has gone away. Life after the marathon does not have to be flat and empty. There are many new directions to take. You may want to consider:

CHAPTER 11

Conclusion

Besides training, having respect for the marathon distance and not forgetting to enjoy the process of getting better is a requirement for a successful and fun marathon. Go for the personal challenge and experience the special event which makes a marathon the trip of a lifetime, that special first time. The basic guidance in this book will prepare you in twelve months from the couch to the starting line of a marathon in a natural and steady way. With enough preparation, you can reach a high level of fitness. However, it does not take all of your time even when your current level of fitness is zero. There are some crucial things to remember: stick to the schedule to avoid getting injured, make sure you get sufficient rest, and do not forget to fully enjoy the running.

As a beginner, the preparation for running a marathon can be a daunting one. Over the past eleven weeks, we have mentally prepared ourselves for a year's worth of work, but with the gradual build-up over a long period of time, the task ahead really wasn't hard. The at times tough training schedule has allowed us to gradually reach our current level of fitness, and with the proper preparation, the running of a marathon was an anticlimax. With the methods as described in this book, you too can run a marathon. You can do it, you will do it with hard work and having a clear schedule in front of you. The structure provided by a good training schedule makes sure you can reach your goal of running a marathon. The schedule is proven and uses the experiences of 28 successful marathon runners and coaches before you.

www.ingramcontent.com/pod-product-compliance
Lightning Source LLC
LaVergne TN
LVHW092100060526
838201LV00047B/1490